james i wanted to ask you

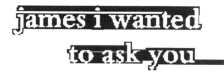

james i wanted
to ask you

michael holmes

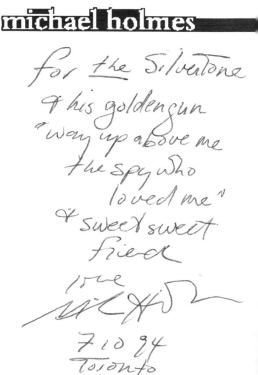

for the Silvertone
& his goldengun
"way up above me
the spy who
loved me"
& sweet sweet
fred

love
mike h
7 10 94
Toronto

ecw press

CANADIAN CATALOGUING IN PUBLICATION DATA

Holmes, Michael, 1966–
    James I wanted to ask you

Poems.
ISBN 1-55022-223-6

I. Title.

PS8565.O56J3 1994   C811 .54   C94-932060-9
PR9199.3.H65J3 1994

altered states have occurred. grateful acknowledgement is made
to *Aria 7*, *Brief*, *Cabaret Vert*, *Ink*, *Oversion*, *Quarry*, *SinOverTan*, &
The Underground Review, where parts of this poem first appeared.

the author would like to thank steven heighton, patricia seaman,
& bruce whiteman for the comments & criticism that helped shape
this book.

front cover photos: d.a. holmes
back cover photo: mary huggard
cover design: stan bevington
typesetting: ecw type & art

james i wanted to ask you has been published with the assistance
of the ontario arts council and the canada council.

the general editor of ecw poetry books is bruce whiteman

printed by coach house printing, toronto, ontario.
published by ecw press, 2120 queen street east,
toronto, ontario m4e 1e2.

Yet once more, O ye laurels, and once more
Ye myrtles brown, with ivy never sere,
I come to pluck your berries harsh and crude,
And with forced fingers rude,
Shatter your leaves before the mellowing year.
Bitter constraint, and sad occasion dear,
Compels me to disturb your season due;
For Lycidas is dead, dead ere his prime,
Young Lycidas, and hath not left his peer.
Who would not sing for Lycidas?. . .

— John Milton, 1608–1674

what else should i be
all apologies
what else should i say
everyone is gay
what else should i write
i don't have the right
what else should i be
all apologies

— Kurt Cobain, 1967–1994

support guidance friendship inspiration & indulgence musterroll:

annex books maria-jesus llarena ascanio bahaus john barlow
stan bevington bill bissett black sabbath christian bök d boon
nancy bullis tony burgess johnny cash cayce the cat douglas
chambers the clash kurt cobain don coles concrete blonde
lynn crosbie chuck d jack david peter day nancy dembowski
christopher dewdney bernd dietz & the universidad de la laguna
ernest the stanza douglas fetherling janet fetherling ian firla
the future doug gilmour & the 1992–1994 toronto maple leafs
thom gunn steven "the source" heighton darren holmes william
& brigitte holmes & the rest of my family mary huggard amanda
huggins hüsker dü the idler pub & staff ilyich's gayle irwin
michael jest daniel jones bill kennedy august kleinzahler
the league of canadian poets beth learn joy learn longhouse
courtney love john lydon carol malyon tom marshall mac
mcarthur don mcleod peter mcphee the meat puppets amanda
mills (artbooks) misfits / samhain / danzig barbara morris
motorhead bp nichol ken norris the ontario arts council keiko
ota parliament (george clinton & p funk) craig paterson jan
pearson & the york university graduate programme in english
the red hot chili peppers rejeanne's country & western laser
karaoke matthew remski the replacements trent reznor jenny &
the riviera stan rogal & bald ego the rollins band heather ross
kelly ryan martha sharpe sshrc ian sowton sugar the tap
suicidal tendencies clive thompson suzy & james townsend
the tragically hip michelle tremblay richard vaughan the velvet
underground death waits tom waits mike watt & fIREHOSE
darren wershler-henry bruce whiteman

& especially patti seaman

for james ohi
1966–1993
&
james mark sebastian townsend
born june 18, 1991

"the wor(l)d is. this ain't."
— james ohi (1984)

(the word is the saint)
— jaymz (1994)

"i go cry now"
— j.m.s. townsend (1994)

(august 7, 1993 — june 18, 1994)
brampton — toronto — winnipeg — medicine hat —
vancouver — stockholm — gothenberg —
athens — naxos — jerusalem — london —
barcelona — toledo — madrid — la laguna —
santa cruz — london — toronto — kingston —
montreal — st. catharines — brampton

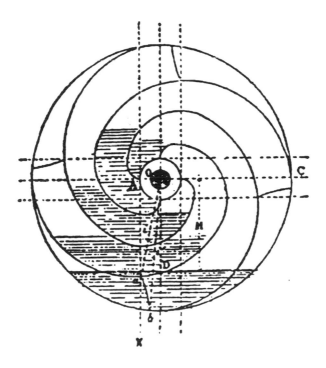

james i wanted to ask you
about your life how falling
in love was what the death
of your mother meant

whether your sisters were ok
instead i trace these vestiges
compulsively feeling common
& ashamed with my shuddas

& cuddas & regrets since
impotence means all i can offer you
is solipsism & apostrophe
the worst & only kind of elegy

i know if that's what this is
i mean my mother was chopping
vegetables & i was making
tasteless brutal jokes

about the way you were killed *destroyed*
roadrunner & coyote allusions
my father thought disgusting —
meep meep splat **poof**

& accordion distortions —
when i opened my notebook
& fucked with the date
involuntarily *writing*

6 8 93
not the day it was
the next day but the day
this should end

this is how it begins **suddenly**
my family goes about itself
as it's always done dinner gets made
a radio bleeds thru the knife

hits the cutting board my father
forgives me numb to how that jackknifed
tractor trailer crushed the breath
out of you & your new wife

but the elegized can't be compacted
you were supposed to drown or contract
tb — aids i guess — not just stop
instantly on a highway outside woodstock

& i am supposed to know you love you
like a brother or more but i don't
& you're supposed to be exemplary
of something anything

there is supposed to be something
to hang on to but there isn't
& i am supposed to be composed
in reconstructing you

tho i'm not because i am
writing for myself in writing for you
james i've never been good
at relating presenting

what i mean without fucking
up — shadowplay sleight
of hand obscurity
& dissimulation

being the best of what i've done
when trying too hard to find
something anything to write
about when i guess i'm trying

to convince someone anyone
that i am a writer or when
fine my ego cons me sometimes
everytime into believing that i am

& now i'm afraid you're gonna
get lost in this
between the absences i'm fixing
between this word & the next

(drinks on peter at the apostle's bar)

"where do bad folks go when they die
they don't go to heaven where the angels fly
they go to the lake of fire & fry
don't see'em again till the 4th of july"
        — curt kirkwood

the sandwich-board
this side of barry's bay
— black&orange alpha-scraps
stuck on yellow ground — says

**gET STrAigHT wiTH yoUr jESUS
And HE ll B STrAigHT wiTH U**
& there's buckets of time
on a milk-run plenty

room to repose
so the bus's disappearing
out the burn of this pitch
goes all pistons & horses

& nodding city dope
having nothing doing
with the retinal discomfort
of truck-stop exegesis

or a side of contact vertigo
next burg we stop in i'm making the call:
"the 20 bucks you spotted us
by tuesday next

or a pitcher & shot at the duke's
when&howmuch what you will"
but before i can fess up
on this twobit roadside box

the sakes of that voice kick:
we're sorry, but peter's number
is no longer in service. . . .
& rock maybe the wires got crossed

but the parable you learn
hangs on the tone:
some folks just can't be told
what they don't wanna hear

what would you say if i told you
that in the last months of your life
i'd taken to thinking of myself
as a kind of frankenstein?

not the creation but the creator
for 3 1/2 years i fantasized
about resurrection shuffling
people piecemeal into the fiction

of a vital communal body
but now my necrophilia
has come back to haunt me
reading these words my monster

will think i'm crazy
it won't like the messianic
lack of artifice critical
acumen & rigour

it won't like you
but because you are dead
because you are rigorous
you are part of it

& this pleases me james i want you
to be part of this world
i want it to know you
because i want to know you

(so i said i love u elat)

from haifa to beer sheva via tel aviv
(this coastline shifting to dunecrests
for supple reclamation & *moshave* plots)
all the signs read: **BEWARE OF SAND**

out of this mirror image
or mimetic rage
they found a shortcut
against the grain

but james i'm afraid of fine crystal
how getting stoned
i'm thrown against the *kotel*
by run(a)way *yeshiva* girls

& the paparazzis' clamour
for what's new this fall
the carmina burana pumping
musakal prednisone

as she trips nostalgic
& i follow the logic
of the null set
to the square root

of language
thru the neurotics
of the looking glass
israel is

(begin again now)

reframed the frame
eloquent essential
refrained from speaking
shifting constituents

according to reb zelig
traffic is blissful
citing authorities
i'm unable to cable

& she's in her *yeshiva*
paying for the bed
& i'm in mine
going out of my head

cutting out letters
closing all **bets**
a chronic syntagm
a narcotic writ

(1000 elegies for peter day: *straight — mayday 1994*)

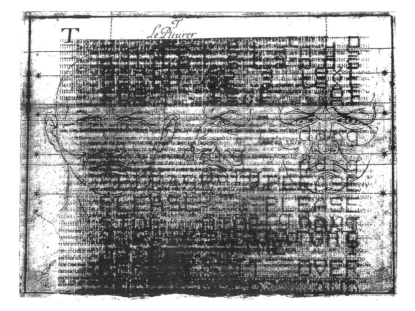

i never saw your hyphen —
won't distinguish pigmentation
to colour a caress —
your eyes were miracles

pitched to pierce
the seamless calculus
of asymptotic skin
or trace vectors

falling subatomic trills
across diminuendo nights
james i've always known
august tin-sheet skies

saw-bow thunderstrafes
the dogs heard first
hart lake & chinguacousy
were convergences like this

dreamscapes we knew
we must not seek
for the disappearance
of them a resonance

in synaesthetic physics
but this harbourfront
luminescence is a single-malt
ghost off curryburnt lips

& i'm drunker than her navigation
& i'm swearing like a sailor
& i feel like a rapist
dancing with these indians

& i can't imagine bombay
let alone goa
& today's the anniversary
of littleboy's murder

applepie genocide
to destroy the diaspora
& i don't remember hiroshima
& i've forgotten nagasaki

like i won't know you're dead
when i fish out my car-keys
& i'll drink this killer kool-aid
then cream for velma's body

because i'm ashamed of what i am
who i become when i'm hungry
say jackal or asshole
say lunatic or psycho

say wile e coyote
& his monstrous fucking ego
because james i wanted to ask you
about the moon tonight

did you notice? was it full?
or occluded? lost in other lights
did you ever let it take control?
did it make *you* afraid sometimes?

(hebrew u)

won't flinch at a b
but when the concrete rocks
& the panes flex
outta this skin

& acutely sensitive
seems appropriate
never gonna be
bored with explosives

how the locals manage
smiles & cappuccino
& forward-thinking
converse

may the whiff
of plastique
or spilt nitro
always alarm me

never wanna be
one to figure
the israeli girl
screaming & twitching

at the little
honey needle
that alights soft
to her near skin

"is it something i said when i lost my mind
temper too quick makes me blind   *i apologize*"
    — bob mould

why you were & what you mean —
i tell somebody how somebody told me:
it's the slope of their eyes
he whispered *no peripheral vision*

& now this mess my stomach is
after 2 ulcers & 2 horrible x-mas scenes
septic after 2 bottles of bushmills
in 3 days: one more fucking *joke* like this

& someone's gonna get dusted —
not a soldier in the cardo
but you lover
(unsuspecting passenger)

you might think you see
the corners & exits & signs
but a suckerpunch comes from nowhere
when you're being taken for a ride

(begin again now again)

james i was in this *yeshiva.*   the boy behind the desk
called himself "ellie."   he was from brooklyn.   he spoke of
"free will" as a binary system.   a body / soul duality.   he
said he could prove that a soul knows "the good" & "the
true" instinctively.   he said that the "soul" once the body
was *disciplined* would make the "right" choice: my soul
got up & left.

it moved to the window & loomed over the dome &
the wall.   it moved to the door & proceeded down the
hall.   it went outside & ordered turkish coffee.   it filled
another pipe & got off on its body.

(terra damnata)

"the space we love is unwilling to remain permanently
enclosed. it deploys and appears to move elsewhere
without difficulty; into other times, and on different
planes of dream and memory."
— gaston bachelard

i take the memorial line
pulling out of union
coast receding loping east
always astonished in recognition

(there is a *coast* to this)
ellipses as landscape
the bluffs whitby oshawa pickering
mnemonics & telling-beads neologisms & mantras

crazy is the 400 miles of steel
that ties me to *rue de st. michel*
tracks my arms to backbeat park
crazy the cat mcphee got at mac's

& wellington in the distance
all schoolhouses & madcows sunflowers & inside dogs
no leash long enough to pull me back
no love longed for like love like that

montreal was nearly the death of me
everything like breath frenched out
almost caught my self in the cold
sense after sense after innocence

sunday dancing the tam tam's tachycardia
tango clots to tarantella strokes
a thornsong under my skin
whiplash smack & flamenco crack

the drug that rhythm is that lies are
montreal half-life of possibility
whistlestop for derailment 200 miles out of sanity
where this thought disembarks thinking

never should have ever left never
never tripped that way never
never kissed those "lips i never should have kissed"
never crossed that bridge never but i did

& paid for it the toll exacted
in memory & lingual dexterity
cns function & respect
& james it's not as bad as things get

i've also taken buses west
hit winnipeg numb to the cut
of chemicals & urine the guys pissed
since sudbury mercifully set

to terrorize portage & main trading
the black woman & her 3 year old son
for new targets *injuns*
one of them said *fuckin injuns*

& i've responded a hundred times
in a hundred different ways
fetishized the confrontation a revenger's tragedy
brandon lee having a real bad day

quentin tarantino's screenplay
john woo's cinematography & exit wounds
a tasteful little flick
the feelgood movie of the summer a surprise hit

but you know the story
we never made it past preproduction
the backers pulled out the director was indicted
for that thing with the 13 year old in a hollywood mansion

no grand jury in the country was gonna buy his story
even if he could prove her mother swore she was 18
makes me feel good tho
to remember it like i took action

like i did the right thing or anything
& didn't regret watching it happen
silent impotent afraid
like i won't always have to torque things this way

& what i have or haven't done could be restaged
like i never woke in medicine hat
thinking christ i could use one
after dreaming your face

thru the climate control & smoked pane
that saved me from the prairies
more a premonition of betrayals to come
than a condemnation of what i've done

how after cheating the terminal
punctuating the forever new westminster is
i put on the put-on & nearly fell
for it myself almost believing

i could be the kind of kitsilano asshole
that's made of other folks' blood & money
(instead of one that's made of where we're from)
until i'd feel the pull of desperation

& cut my teeth again
on the syncopation
of pender & east hastings
cause i'm downtown & shooting

the amber burning hell i am
out **hot l** windows
on some grrrls black wings
above the *army & navy* or *save-on meats*

all tattoos & piercings & restraints
stainless steel courtesy of wilkinson sword
soundtrack by peter murphy trent reznor & flood
scalpels on the cuttingroom floor

because james i won't drive
a computerized fibreglass coffin
don't want no jive
spaceaged bastardization

i need a real
engine of destruction
vintage detroit 440
chrome headers leather interior

an early 70s dodge challenger
late 60s mustang or chevy nova
before the unions & import invasion
something starsky & hutch or the mod squad

would career around in
an indestructible pig
that says "put up or shut up"
& "don't tread on me"

the kind of car john's windsor is
so unlike this gentrified vancouver granola
this groovy temple of affirmative payola
this hologram love-in of virtual pistons

a car with fully functional backseat
& godly fm radio the kind that could get me
past commercial & down main to graveley
back to cayce's turf & the backporch

where the cops would roust me & kelly
for listening to the pogues & laughing quietly
back to barlow for pints at the avanti
all magic in our missives then

madwords & love & visceral stands
the possibility that innocence was that we were
but cayce don't live here no more
he purrs uneasy in a basement on borden

& i'm on these train tracks & hopping freights
walking not driving heading west again
with a guy who'd soon as kill me
as call me his friend

cross fields worth a fortune
once they're salted & damned
ground that we'll sell
to the pacific rim

the same ground upon which
50 years ago james
both you & the moneymen
would have been murdered or interned

because even tho you're a canadian you'd have been a jap first
& no citizenship or birth certificate no protest or legality
would have saved you from our history at its worst
not d-day but dresden not liberation but death camps

& i'm afraid
i repeat the infamy
by trying to fix
what you "mean"

i know i have no right
to write like this james
but the pain your absence leaves
doesn't feel like appropriation

no i want to remember you
because as kids we had everything
in common because i didn't notice
you were "different" when we studied

for mr. hassan's physics exam
or ran the greenbelts in the rain
because i want to remember
how my mother

would transpose your name
to say i got a call
from mr. o-hi-o
how your voice hung there

in our home
"a nip in the air"
before i learned what racism was
how inbred our bigotry is

& james i wanted to ask you
if you'd forgive me this
but i can't because
everything's different

& nothing's changed
& i'm on the rails
heading for a house
that's not my home

where the bed shatters
these candy windshields
because i roll & spoil
the contradictions

pace & waste
fragile eternities
picking her barbs
from what i hide

because on thursdays
the laundry's done
so there's noone else
to gang up on

because i'm reduced to this
playing mr. dressup
whipped tho gentile
in a rich fuck's clothes

because james i've let myself be composed
by someone else's fiction
become a posterboy for self-abnegation
the kind that'll crucify an ego like mine

one that takes what montreal was instinctively
& sometimes gets crushed by the simple cruelties
of queen street those that remind me
i'm not beautiful or wonderful or loving & strong

& that maybe noone wants or will ever need me
that i'm not anything i've pretended to be
how sometimes a smile will peal
ripping into fangs of laughter

& shatter what i was & all that i'm after
when a beautiful woman doesn't look *at* but *thru* me
& i loose this persona & what's cool & easy
& i become my raw self again

the boy walking the dog walking the boy
13 years old awkward mangy
sensitive to the light
& the girls' ridicule

trapped in this body
but not yet vampiric or shifting
a cipher to the sunflower
that hunts me with its cryptonite

not yet a heliotropic *übermensch*
claustrophobic & lisping
afraid to bite off the lie
i'm living tonight

& james for 15 years
i've been hearing the laughter
from schoolyards to nightclubs
i've been stalked by this terror

& i know the sunflower's beautiful
but its seeds will kill me
& i can't discriminate between fears
because allergies are everything

& "just because you're paranoid
doesn't mean that they're not after you"
is more logical than lyrical
& less reduction than reaction

& i'm riding this train east now
back to someplace near sanity
200 miles from montreal
200 miles from your memory

how i've left my past in vancouver
with my wolfsbane & vanity
like i'm leaving toronto for kingston
to get back to steve & mary

.

& the house on johnson
where i first struggled with oxygen
& ripped at my clothes
where i learned to love

running red lights
in a car built for poetry
the *stanza* steve drove
to get me to *hotel dieu*

before i choked on my words
& the sunflower in the chili
& james i'll never forget
how a friendship saved my life that night

like i'll never forget
dancing & talking with tom
— after the needle brought me back —
just months before he died

because the sunflower will take me
the sunflower's a killer
because the sunflower's inside me
a sunflower's the lover

pulsing spanish thru these arteries
whispering *sweet suicide epinephrine?*
you don't need adrenaline
what you want dear michael is peace

(11 11 93 jerusalem)

parched behind barbs
interred in the negev
saying tanks
with lasers that cut

thru dust unbroken:
"me & the wife left hoboken
— retired to lovely miami fla. —
& my buddy's got the patent

on this device
& i'm here to give it
to these israelis
& you're young & never been to war

but i'm here to tell you
no body wins no body
because i was in this bus
back in las vegas

just me & a million
japanese tourists —
so i told'em christ
i killed you people

& you know what they said?
'well we're *here* now'
& that's just it
you got a cross *here*

& a jewish star *there*
& all my pals dead
& i was killing
innocent people

these hands
were killing
innocent
people"

("in the land of the blind the one-eyed man is king"
— *singapore*)

i am a rainbow
i am a warrior
i am a gypsy
my soul will never die

when we got in the jeep at wadi farqan
so unseasonably hot even for the desert
i thought it's definitely not an oasis this place
even your piss evaporates instantly

it doesn't hit the ground
& you actually don't sweat
tho all the water's sucked out
you're really bone dry

like you're already decomposed
worse than buried alive
growing skeletal & nothing
at the same time

& then you sat in the soldier's lap
& lied about your age
& we passed some naked warriors
showering & he held you & said

now she has a nice body don't you think
& my head bounced off the rollbar
& my back was aching
sitting between an uzi & an m16

barrels to me
on top of the military radio
& we were dehydrated
& i watched his wet surge

feeling you
& *your* near skin
beside him
& i let this go thru me

enjoying the power you had in this place
nomadic more than the desert
more than this hell
& i remembered squatting

that tent beside our daycamp
the precious little shadowplace
we occupied near delirium
fucked after boomshanka

& drinking 6 gallons
of dysentery each
— the rainbows that we talked:
how moses cudda come

thru that pass after 30 days
& rested *his* blistered & infected feet
upon this very rock his hands
swatting the same diseased flies

his eyes waiting out the tedious decline
of the same vicious sun —
& then my skull really cracked
the pipe hard again

& i thought jesus
my head's gonna split wide
& if we roll this thing
on this terrain

then first my right leg
will snap in two
& then one of their guns
is gonna discharge

& put a fucking hole
the size of a fist
right thru the middle
of my chest

& then the jeep stopped
under the flag
by the kitchen
& you skipped out

so light so magical
to find our sleeping bags
& towels
& the soldier who was

soaking you in
turned to me & asked
if i had *suffered*
— more cynical & disgusted

than your patience could allow
— him hating me looking like a freak
in tartan rainbow filth
hair long & dreaded

sand in every orifice
& i know how badly
he wanted me
to *suffer*

an eternity
for being so
intimate
with your beauty

& how hateful he was
when i said
no man   i loved it
the desert is so "ragin"

so beautiful   so wonderful
so not like canada   like home
& then you skipped back
& we took off again

a little more angrily
& i thought of the dope in my pocket
& the picture we must make
the wonderful polarity sparked

by the contrast of our colour
against this drab olive ground
all four of our bodies pressed
into this tiny space

& even tho i was *suffering*
the heat & this crushing
claustrophobia
i was so happy

watching the freaks
& flies & dunes recede
so happy to be free
in this military vehicle

with you
& when my head
smashed the bar
for the last time

just over the bridge
mcphee twice broke
& the stars danced
behind my eyes again

& we were on a road
in the middle of noplace
going one way to elat
& the other to beer sheva

i was so bursting
out of that jeep
that small place
getting so much taller

& then i watched you take
the cool strawberry yogurt
from his rough hands
so delicate so innocent

never figuring he could be
one of two reservists who'd *suffer*
the most inhumane torture
before the assassin's bullet

kisses thru his eye
& the jerusalem post says
mirage becomes carnage
as the desert sun sets

(medicine hat my head's splitting)

(ein gedi)

thinking these racist thoughts
so full of blessings
& the oasis waterfall
still clinging to my body

naked in it
cleansed of the dysentery
impossibly re-hydrated
unbalanced & shifting now

swaying slightly to the right
shalom i've always leaned
the other way *shalom*
they always say

shalom here *shabbat shalom*
good *shabbas*
everyone says welcome home
baruch ha shem

the freaks & the rebbes
welcome home
in english or hebrew
welcoming me home

the armenians & money changers
the chuk & st. michel café
this is home welcome
welcome home

james i wanted to ask you
how you remembered me
did you know we'd never
see each other again? did you

believe that it would happen by a lake
or in a loblaws or filling up
the tank of your yellow tercel?
was it pleasant but awkward

with a how the hell are you
or christ it's been 10 years?
was i with a lover & did you
have a daughter who was almost

afraid of me? days later
did you phone your dad
& just to make conversation say
you ran into mike? did you

have to explain who mike was?
did i tell you a lie you
thought was the truth? did we
say we'd keep in touch but forget

to get a number? did we touch
each other at all? did it make
you think? did it mean *anything*?
i'm asking because i'm remembering

everything i can't remember
(i have to think about you)
i have to force myself to relocate you
someone something that might be you

in high school everyone you half know dies on friday or
saturday night — they shoot themselves in the head with
their father's hunting rifle or they take acid & lock
themselves in their brother's van at 3 am with a power
tool capable of taking off a hand & bleed to death —
gracefully if pitifully — drowned in the buzz of
shimmying teeth. or maybe they augured a lifelong
struggle between workaday & the weekend & necktie
themselves to the visiting team's goal-posts. most often
tho they buy it in groups on the backroads — lose
control on a stretch of treacherous curves — coming
home from the party thru the glorious fog or over the
mysterious black ice.

(6 8 93)

1 beer descent 1 scotch 2 scotch circle brood
2 beer 3 scotch wallow doubt construct 3 beer
4 scotch wait surge forget some more
walk the harbourfront knolls prod

thru the throb of indians sitars guitars
thumbnail rhythms tar barrels
smouldering perfect doughs spices rising
searching for her in the claws of bhangra & boys swarming

i put some personality down my throat
unhinged this jawbone to swallow some pride
she says she's seen noone drink like this
she says it makes me better & worse

what i lose is accountability & acumen
what i gain is sharp tympanum
& i'm perfectly capable of legendary patience
& i want the pain waiting is

& the minute hand's a ritual shiv
& i want the pain waiting is
& her body appears & so does his
& i want the pain waiting is

("vampires winter on greek island" — *weekly world news*)

about the sun with weapons
close to your tongue
leeching secrets cut
on eyeteeth & midnight

how spurious is serious
in serial assaults
not the falconer
immolated vicarious

but the boy i was on naxos
phlegmatic anaemic myopic
almost invisible
patient in the shadows

waiting out dusk for my time
when your heaven's put out
& the moon & the tidebreak
are full up on flesh

pitched in deep choler
gasses pink in my lungs
i can feel it off its tether:
what i am come ripping

"don't you know there ain't no devil
there's just god when he's drunk"
— tom waits

saw terry first james sloped terry slack
terry terry dear terry sidle off the bikepath **(thinking
where is she)** terry diminuendo his blush
to conceal a secret frame terry loping

your body doubled dreams of shrinking
disoriented features ideogrammed softness lockstepped terry
(but where is she) his voice thru the notes of spice
his accusing finger in the curry raga the klieg's

glare off his perfect tan *she follows me*
saw terry first james pissed feral james bent this side
of lycanthropy picked him out of the pacing
stalking the harbourfront perimeter

kingwolf salivating transfixed on the jugular
saw terry first james thinking blunt objects thinking skinteeth
not hiroshima not tractortrailers not anniversaries or jackknives
not you your new wife or what's left of your life

(cyprus)

"i keep my eyes wide open all the time
i keep the ends out for the tie that binds
because you're mine i walk the line"
    — charles manson citing johnny cash

james this is confirmed by the gunshop
greek does turk does greek
rifles / pistols semi or fully automatic
crossbows grenades anti-personnel devices

enjoy diet coke marlboro mcdonald's
jurassic park & bart simpson:
give cyprus a break, man
& we were just eating the local chicken

& i couldn't finish without noticing
people buying weapons smiling
right there beside us
so happy so peaceful

here's the longhand of smiles
on queen street:
(not the accountable
algebraic smiles

of bay street not the bisecting
lingual smiles
of bloor not even
a gloss on

the hard lupine smiles
of yonge street)
             just plum lips
bust up on
        pulling you
              in

(toledo)

i need the infection where
lung & languor
pull thru my throat
in fists of anger
& break into indiscretion:

how you correct my pronunciation
in a language we don't use
when this soft tongue wants
dancing & frustration & curves

treacherous fuckin curves
like the impossible coast
from the arc between your hips & breasts
to the invitation coming on thru your lips
for someone stuck on the wet
                              catch
of the midnight within you

when you are the whole of the love i'm in
my body's translation of houdini's dislocation
the absence into which i almost fit
an excuse for abnegation a pocket

a chamber a capsule an asylum
& i feast on the spanish that walks around me
the children who occupy the zocodover at dusk
this word for more that one for less

& another to forgive my stubbornness
or incomprehensibility & i want
the easy that falls out of them
the little brats who are pulsing

in the ridiculous class of this toledo
mcdonald's whose words for grimace
& hamburgler are still rarefied
& so much more violent than my own

whose lips & teeth still catch the tain
of smoked glass in certain likeness
not yet a colourless compost of curls
or grey wreath of nicotine dissimulation

not yet anaemic or acid-tongued
not yet vampiric abysmal conceited damned
then james you are never dead
tho you may be **suddenly** past revision

james i've been left to these devices
— not quite my own but fortuitous
my second-hand libido this borrowed life
duplicitous in a couple of doubles

your obit begins **suddenly**
it begins that way & this
begins that way this experience
it begins that way twice

& i'm gratefully caught in the paradox
of reading it as it is suddenly
suddenly i'm reading as suddenly
you're dead suddenly

your death is textual & suddenly
i'm suddenly participating
in its texture as suddenly
i'm reading the word suddenly

which suddenly means death
tho suddenly the word no longer looks
like suddenly because
suddenly suddenly takes forever

to be read as suddenly
it defers & suddenly
suddenly becomes perpetual
& suddenly i'm wondering

if it didn't begin suddenly
if it began another way this experience
even if obits always begin suddenly
because death is suddenly not sudden at all

suddenly it's painfully slow
tho i've heard many thank god
that you did not suffer that
you went together instantly —

i've mumbled these words myself
maybe 20 30 times
but it took you 27 years to die
as many years as i've been alive

(bramalea limited)

"i like crazy people, especially those who don't see
the risk"
         — john lydon

the premier & his boys manufactured us muppets: a
bramalea ltd. reality where an alphabet of infernal sesame
streets spell whole subdivisions.

in nightmares it's their buddy paul, the more
mephistophelian of the moguls (the one that reminds me
of a megalomaniacal, paper-clip hording bert), whose
speculation relentlessly constructs the letter-of-the-day in
a viral pinwheel (your childhood, michael: brought to you
by the letters O & Y & the number 666.)   it was a
"planned community," the blueprint stolen from dante:
see, the residential inner circles feed the industrial
perimeter. . . .

bramalea is the kind of cosmic joke you can play on
200,000 or so middle-class folks — one that only *mr.
snufflupagus* or *captain poetry* could fully appreciate.

i lived in the E section.   on earnscliffe circle.   just off
earl's court.   one up from edinburgh.   in bramalea,
geography is *very* important.   at bss, my high school, there
were those from as far away as avondale & balmoral.   an
interesting fact: you can fit the first five letters of the
alphabet into about four square miles.   (now there's
something your primer won't teach you: it's not quite a
1:1 ratio.)

bramalea means that douglas coupland is never gonna *be* the "voice of the X generation." we might produce a few cool-looking books — lots of black, complementary colours, great design — but nothing that'll ever catch, nothing truly *popular.*

ever since watergate was broadcast to the sticks it's been impossible to be urbane. there are stories from the 50s & 60s that older writers can still get away with, but for the most part you've gotta accept that kids who grew up on the children's television workshop & movies about nam — a classic film genre & the only one created by a US president — are gonna cringe at fond reminiscence. still, i figure someone should write about bramalea (we called it viet bram & brampuchia), especially the libelous bits: the best of it all being the damp corduroy headiness about her — allison in jodhpurs — always game for a dry hump. cause if there's nothing deliciously cosmopolitan going for rubick's cube, duran duran, or roller disco you can still make it by japan's "adolescent sex": how the you that you are never looks as ridiculous as those people in group shots nostalgia dresses up.

bramalea is like this. sometimes the radio gets into your clothes: but it's noticeable only after you've gone cold turkey.

bramalea is when you erase all the pre-sets & the best lies come sweetly: how the car shimmied with the weight of fast friends & classes ditched; when savings-time meant a summer boon of 1/2 bag highs cheap & demented, the kind that work up the glow of immortal teen-aged night-sweats & the ABCs of cruising the streets with *grover & cookie.*

bramalea is about how there are two kinds of people in the world.

it's simple: you either *choose* to be an *ernie*, or you're gonna be a *bert*.

james it's funny people are forever
making me read things
— an occupational hazard
i guess it's what i do now

how i get myself jacked —
they tell me to check out books
strangers' books
friends' books

their own books
novels poems theory
technical manuals cookbooks pornography
hell i even read subway posters

recreationally so it's not exactly surprising
that i was told where
to read about you
my mom's friend anne from work

she reads the births & deaths page
religiously just to check that she
hasn't died unexpectedly
she read about you in the star

divined it (section A) on the 9th
& she told my mother
who then told me all it took was
50 cents & i found you **suddenly**

suddenly after seven years 2 1/2 degrees
a marriage & the paperwork for a divorce suddenly
i was back taking refuge waiting
patiently pretending to be patient

haunting the rooms that you knew
as my home for 3/4s of our lives
suddenly waiting waiting
for something anything to happen

waiting for the fall in brampton
waiting out the summer re-learning
my family waiting weighing
their routines against my rejections

— this desire beside that —
waiting waiting for repercussions
the tenor of shame waiting
knowing that in time this too

must close suddenly waiting on a woman
i thought i loved patiently waiting
for her acceptance discovering
in her who i was & why

weighing her desire with mine
waiting waiting out the temper
of this & mine my temper
waiting patiently suddenly weighing

the measure of a word like death
& suddenly i'm faced by the inconsequence
of what i construct these letters
& scenarios this one & the next

obsessed with the fade into
violent depression blurred reception
silent dispersion this viral imprecision
almost about you

when i remember nothing but that i should
& you don't register except in the ghosts
lingering sense memories thru
temporal amputations

how a hockey bag smells
in the back of dad's gremlin
or the cool of still damp gloves
& easing leather

the hiss my *supremes* made
cross-cut over their blue
& into the slot
& i wanna call you soft-hands

or "heady" & quick
make you into a theo fleury
or killer gilmour
tough & before their time

but hockey was still a mugs game
without teflon stars
anabolic or turbo-charged
& we played broadstreet bullies

in the circle or between the cars
scraping palms & knees
blocking shots with comic-book body parts
how when some guy on the other team

would actually kick at me
blades first & all
i'd take my stick upside his head
& get away with it

cause i was big
& lived up the street
from the ref
the one with the sister

who three years later
gave me the best
birthday gift
i'd ever get

james you are receding
i've lost the pulse the pain
the initial sequence the evidence
wanting to communicate

with you thru you to you
being effaced by the incompatibility
of language & stability
(desire & logic) blood types

because the calendar
because the final end rhyme
because the first smoke & coffee
because i can't stop reading

the figure in the ground
in which you were interred —
meeting deadlines
by throwing out lifelines —

eliding shovel & soil
with paper & pen
(chisel & marble)
refuse & refusal

this terrible pun
this k(not come undone
i'm washing over you
spilling into the gaps

that were you my grip
this last grasp slips
& there's precious little
to hang on to

except the notes i wrote
to remind myself of you
cryptic tags i appended
to the back of your first draft

anatomical mementoes pathological
notations dentals as identification
the distorted sound bites
the random digital samples

that replay you your voice
& smile disembodied your fingers
finding the black keys
a requiem while the wind

howled december 1983
this air telling me all i know
about you & what i do not know
of tedium of repetition

james i wanted to ask you
about your life how falling
in love was what the death
of your mother meant —

whether you could teach me
to forget & forgive
whether i'm doing the right thing
by you for you to you

because this is about shifting
positions not being stable
how at the kitchen table
i pulled on another cigarette

& made myself drift
in all i had a right to
the remarkable newness the difference
that your death meant

what doesn't matter is
all the others all the ones
i did not cry for those i knew
shared with or loved for those

whose absence was tangible almost real
something opened inside shattered
i was culpable it was personal
this implicated me where i'm from

i don't know you & i should
know you there are things
i should have done i said
to her clutching my body

you went to spirit
without a thought for me
like **daniel & peter**
without a thought for me

"accidents are almost predatory in this universe"
    — christopher dewdney

minus 1 friend
minus 1 name
minus 1 memory more
a world without you

not necessarily a world without you
still on this track still pending
no remarkable difference
nothing remarkable at all

except this stillness this sameness
so furious & driving
too fast & persistent without you
how each subtraction leaves less

space for me making manoeuvrability
more difficult burning off the oxygen
that fuels this machine preserving
only temporal fissures

on these murderous curves driving
this livid remainder racing
ovoid futile horrified wide-eyed
confronted by the warning

objects are closer than they appear
transfixed in the headlights'
animal onslaught
the speeding pulse near recognition

before your seething lapse into resignation
this face defaced
in pathetic aphasia
compressed in the crush of

certain steel wrenched
thru shattered pane
as wheelstocks rip
gutwrought skin

diluting spectral absence
to deceptive translucence
thin & insignificant
almost illegible

a flatline cut in marble block
almost merely a minus
a deletion almost a paraph slashed —
nothing more

how the clearing of this space
constricts & restricts
my content my form minus
my self-possessed obsession minus

my friend minus
my name minus
1 minus
more

every possible stimulus catching
shepherded pulling up
another thread
every direct & easy thought

becoming wrapped & warped
cloaked in my complex
this impossible lapse
misread as wilful

digression & james
even this evasion
caressing whatever thought
was first meant

kicks at my sense
wanting to make nice
or be wonderful
wanting to be beautiful

& loving & strong
how clean would just be
the way it was meant to mean
& i wouldn't waste a lifetime

waiting out the links
or most evolved acknowledgement
because it was music translated
into spanish & her terrified

response to a streetfreak
while trying to enjoy breakfast
that started it
focused this procrastination

when between every conceivable play
her ability to get things done
pulls me into my impossibility
— how i should be writing this poem

or that letter or at least a request
— how it should be simple & removed
— how it should be so unlike me
that it might appear to be the truth

(4 10 93 stockholm)

james give me a sign
to fix you in this
messianic semiotics:
make it all better

for a poor pissed libra
who wants to annex his cosmology
in the flesh equity
of elke the SAS stewardess

james i've tried to efface you
fled 6000 miles to erase you
left you undone. . .

(barcelona)

"burn the church from the spire
make your bed a big briar. . .
you fuckin pay for desire. . .
thorns of chemical wire"
            — mike watt

dynamic she said
— shattered daily —
waking warm near her
cooling to the room

absorbing tensions & tensors
full up in them
& the character of my dead friend
asserting insinuated between us

no other voice penetrating
this sediment concrete sentimental
another fucking café
for you to fade into

(route 66)

wanting to talk with peter
about classic american jazz stylings
— 20s 30s 40s —
great female vocalists whose names

are simply legendary tags
i really should know more about:
but it's the way her voice skirts
the bass line — scatting round

thicknesses —
words like missouri
magical words
all molasses or gumbo

women with chords like bourbon
who're only similes for my ignorance
— these sounds so near to ones my mind makes
— ones i dream of getting nearer to

& i'm in this madrid café
of some historical import i guess
all chipped marble
& low pressure fronts

bookcase aquariums
swimming with yellowing firsts
titled *Tres Poetas. . .*
Tres Palabras & *El Abuelo*

feeling almost lucid
behind the tension train
separating me from my lover
& there's a cello doubling the melody

& peter would know whose voice this is
could probably say what label she was on
& who was her tenor
or how that sound got made

on that guitar
before effects pedals
& it's not that i miss the fucker
4000 miles away

it's just that it makes me feel right to think
of the friend who hugged me when i fell to pieces
in his small place on palmerston
just about a year ago

this guy who broke my nose twice in three weeks
& could both laugh & write
a real fine poem about it
a gift for his friends

& it's good to know he's probably dreaming right now
— maybe beside you —
after a hard night of living
sleeping off a saturday anticipating

waking on coronation street
or putting on the gloves & sweats
for some hardheaded shinny
with *his* childhood & refusal to grow old

rick threw this floater hailmary
got stuck on the sun breaking out
of thanksgiving shadowcast
all epiphanic hangtime

dean cutting to cover duffy's brother fading
me pushing by any reasonable button-hook
25 30 yards
christ duff had an arm

& i felt the rope that tied the bomb to my palms
& james crunching the last leaves chase down my flank
& i felt the sky hand the ball back
when james tripped on his own grace & speed

& i thought rick & me steamboat kings
too close to indiscretion to see
how ineffable completion is
too young to account for chaos

too big with immortality to catch
the majestic treachery of immanence
— how the random mechanics of failure
always come out to play

(tenerife 1)

mapmaker mapmaker make me a map

tracing the alleys of your disgust
thru the calles of la laguna
picking up on a cerveza (here & here)
avoiding the shit & howling
but never never seeing a dog

beautiful women everywhere before xmas
drinking tall aguas in the cafés
doing xtc & sloe whisky grinds in the clubs
always with beautiful friends
but never never with men

i feel the young ones — 17 18 maybe —
sizing up my hands: **eh**soft she said
y mui caliente — always aspirating her shift
to **eh**spanish
           but it's a sneaky rain falling
& even lingual dexterity can't keep it up

(what's the use getting wet if you can't enjoy the pun?)
closure this exotic is a rare & precious gift
— i couldn't script a more fitting end —
when you're this hard freedom is fetish
& i thank you you have **untied me** & *my* insanity

"who the hell you calling crazy? you wouldn't know what
crazy was if charles manson was eating fruit loops on your
front porch"
          — mike muir

in madrid this superhero poem for mcphee started
pushing thru the copper tabletops & sheetmetal placemats
— real heartfelt & jazzy — till i got edgy
with the thought of sitting in the wake of your displacement

so james i overcompensated by fetishizing transformations
like the adrenaline that makes a *bill bixby* a *lou ferrigno*
& i wondered how all that green make-up felt under the klie{
& i thought it must have been a hell of a lot like this

the procession before us
everyone yours closer than me
my shoulderroll knucklecrack my craning
to con the coffins twins

another couple of doubles teratoid
sleeping snake-eyed
my vision dilated with
the shuffleweight weddingstep

two-by down the incline
but i'm looking to transcend
the funereal tempo & the way the wail
your wife's mother made resonated

where fundamentalists might pitch
a kind of deep-fried altar sublime
her anguish a worse fix
than getting this religion is

drano harmonics cutting my carotid
every synapse collapsed
the waiting catharsis
wondering how badly fucked

a body has to be
before they deny the hunger
that mourning has for closure
that i have for beauty

or love eternal whatever the deformity
& james i've known a woman
paralysed by disease & disorder
dysfunction & misfortune

made me feel more a freak than "the freaks"
she bled my compassion from
led me to learn to forget
to "let the ugly in"

to forget where i've been
the monstrosities i've made
the shameful things i've done
willingly how i've caused real pain

& could do so again subtly
if not sadistically but james
i'm standing by the last pew
in your church standing with my father

hiding every scar & tattoo
with a tie & suit
cloaking discomfort respectfully
behind black & blue

behind borrowed empathy
i've got a photograph
to document the event
that she took of me

earlier this evening
my father & i grinning
hideous irreverent obnoxious
more a rite of passage shot

than a parting shot
has a right to be
my smile betraying the crimes
i've committed against memory

the way i forgot another
in the life i chose
the way i forgot you
because you weren't cool

to hang around with anymore
the way i forgot you
because i had to be the anomaly
(punk poet student freak)

because james i had to be cool
had to be because if you're not cool
you're not anything or so i believed
tho i know now it was not cool

this belief & that i'm not cool
& never have been & i also know finally
that there can be no apology
(tho i may be more "sorry"

than all this fucking self-pity)
more regretful than the calculated
murder of what you meant to me
the time we spent dreaming

on the rockets we made
that made your father cry tonight
the ones we sent after the possibility of life
suffering that bastard mr. fridkin's class

for the burn of small explosions
& a chute that might open
or not the dreams your father
built for you that i blessed was there for

or skating with you james gary
with a whistle blowing stops & starts
how i think i'm blowing these fits
angry over some loss

to a team we should have beat
your breathing heavy but more effortless
& understanding than my own
but now it's gary pacing not skating slowly

ahead of me mabel & brian too
suddenly they've reached your coffin stopped
& started into the wings as i now do
suddenly after discovering what i've contorted

for what i've craved the photo of you
on your wedding day your love
easy intense beautiful
& it's you james not me you're cool

always have been & tho i know
i'll never get to hang with you
i'm remembering now to remember memory
to forget forgetting how i used to be

(9 poems about yesterday)

I.

angle of desire: the arc grooved in the rails pitch.
tracking her treacherous curves he rode her to anonymity.

2.

she forked out my i with her happy valentines.

3.

    set tween the crescents of your pornographics the curve
i've spun on your square brackets lies the secretary of the
unconscious.

4.

the best bumper sticker i've ever seen says "my canada includes uranus."

5.

imagine my surprise: i went to the corner to buy smokes & milk & discovered a photograph of my missing inner child printed on the carton. it was a school picture-day shot, grade 4 or 5, computer altered to age. i didn't recognize him immediately, but i'd know that wide-collared pink polka-dotted shirt anywhere. i called the 1-800 number, asked for an 8 x 10 glossy, breathed heavily & beat into the carton.

6.

jesus wept.   i resolved to greet a sick & twisted fuck
with a sick & twisted fuck.

7.

in her megalomaniacal desire for gastronomical purity i discovered she was a vegetaryan.

8.

swell.   a stormcloud bust-up a notoriously bad tattoo a
coffeemate pretention to a favourite café a spiked
suckerpunch a combine a silo a miniskirt of questionable
intent a steeple a **stylo** a smelted vowel movement a
healthy rejection of irony a franco-phonebill a blackshirt's
love of tapestry a dada déjà vu a scintillating picket line of
tired pickup lines a veritable popcornucopia a pinter play
a winter slay a hinterland whose hoo.

9.

his timing impeccable, he pulled out & spunked a thick stream of bubbling jizz over her tits & onto her face — actually realizing his lifelong dream of cuming into a startled open eye. miraculously, she accepted tourette's as an excuse for his idiosyncratic behaviour.

10.

i'm a libidinal band.   i'm coming to your town.   i'm
gonna party you down.   i'm a libidinal band.

(13 2 94)

timor mortis conturbat me

whether you were in the end
matters little we had much in common
the chinese furrows your books made
a thing for motorhead waits & nico

a vested interest in control & kaos
janet sweet janet all wisdom & beauty
a curio sadness & pop culture fetish
(a life touched by *this* disease)

men's fashion mags & the cruelty betrayed
women subjected to abomination unfathomable
spaces marked with feral obsession
the rage for order of one possessed

ends that frayed & friends that
split (or stayed) these things i recognized
eased into your chair muscles blossomed
blue against your stairs the tedium

that dispersion is that effects are
your telephone in my bag ringing
the ghost of me ringing peter
4 years ago his voice in the machine

provoking my irate message let down & stood up
wondering where in the hell he was
why he didn't make the meeting
why he didn't at least call

& i remember joining chris for dinner
at that nicaraguan place north of keiko's
an hour after craig phoned to say
they'd taken peter's body

& i remember how i couldn't cry
until i started on the chivas
& i know my friends thought the scotch
might never stop but it did

tho the ringing didn't & this time
it's robyn answering & tony on the line
& i'm dreaming lynn & patti
their love that i love

& the world is closing in on this poem
because it's james i'm calling now
his number already disconnected
& yours soon out of service

so noone's holding a gun to my head
& i sure don't need another drink
but i want the scotch tonight —
the sweet metallic bite of its amber suicide —

& i'm thinking i might be insane
listening to nirvana's "lithium"
& defining death in depression
(always touched by this disease)

but i'm drunk enough to convince myself
that i know everyone tho i didn't know you
& have no right to write like this
because i didn't know you at all

tho i am drunk enough to repeat myself
to be a sick & twisted fuck —
to actually plug in *your* phone
& give *you* a call

because i wanted to tell you
about this poem what the death
of james meant about the way it might
end by never ending at all

(bramalea city centre)

4 months from where love was where i am
suddenly reckoning on this accounting for
what i must do with body & mind —
when annotation is waiting

& i'm a journal or anecdote
& you've been this far
since we were close
i distinguish the blessings

i engaged for you
from the things i think
i was expected to do
i make this apparatus my own

(st. catharines)

what you are sleeping (softer than your nightlight your
mother beautiful always beside me always beside you)
your mother's son

fair explosive tempered down curl that dream is the only
being breathing breathing livid innocent of all possible
play

exhausting language for the lie of its newness how
nothing can't happen when you tether the pitch & you're
almost three & you know what you love

in everything you are you are everything

& i want to hold this breath forever in your laughter the
way you held me & whispered *my michael don't be sad*
quiet thru the chaos my life was to bring me home to
your peace & love

& you are small & will live forever like this knowing
knowing simply knowing every sacred memory defiant &
perfectly complete speaking & knowing *i'm not your baby
i'm james*

(for *mt*)

"love is the vampire drunk on your blood"
    — johnette napolitano

moon shivs thru blind cascades
hunk off hacked beams to
shimmy down on passion

wanting to say your smell on me
wanting to compass flash geomancy
& whereabouts sweet lineaments off hidden curves

but i'm stuck on trying to lukacs this
step on what busts out the vague wash:

amber dancing crabapple from crystal
cobalt ashtray perilous on a canary pencil hinge
dried vermilion downsided, crucified
   on the little blackhaired girl's canopy
the black curls of the little blackhaired girl herself
herself at the wedge the black typer is
the alabaster & charcoaled shadow of the skin of one leg
the nightshade enveloping her hips
the denim fade of her boy's shirt
the silver spell thru her lower lip

& i float up her cumulous down
& i whisper while she works

but i'm no painter & this ain't even
a first kiss or sideways caress

& her bed is lit with rainbows & steel
funereal roses & heather
telling candles as incantations

& i would dream her(e to resolution
& she would fit my sleep like this

start across my arm & tuck
her breath rolling upon my neck

(tenerife 2)

dying was better
tho i don't remember much
but the softness falling
down falling enveloping me

my throat closing round
simple acknowledgements
my breathless part
lips busting eyes swelling shut

tongue growing into my mouth
as the girl allergic to the sea
made the sad elision
from heliotrope to seed

& i had to stagger & reach
for the first needle in years
calm for the comic in it
how i could explain irony finally

between objectivity & death

& i was alone
& i was crying thru the burning
& the only sound i could make
sounded like your name

& i was on the floor struggling with oxygen
& i was ripping at my close
& i was going to die as i was going to love you
between the stench & the filth

& i knew what to do
& i stuck myself

& it hurt less than being alive

(eulogy: a few more last words)

not even a year has passed.   james ohi died on a beautiful,
serene night last august.   that much i remember (i think).
it was warm.   humid maybe.   in toronto there was a
festival of east indian music & culture.   harbourfront:
curry, raga, drinking, dancing.   me?   i was the guy
slurring the chorus to the clash's "choose the right
profile" & johnny cash's "ring of fire."   more than a bit
snapped.

fuck lola's lounge: i should've been at a karaoke bar.

in brampton the next morning, at my parents' breakfast
table, i was told that james was dead.   a few hours later i
began this poem.   then i left canada.   travelled & wrote
some more.   i returned & continued.

other friends have died.   too many.

& the pitch of relationships has also been transposed.
(these are the destroyed.)   like too much msg: the
penultimate fortune cookie said "you will experience
change for the better."   but it's the last that's become my
alltime favourite: *it was empty.*   (i'm learning.)   got no
fortune at all. . . .

but it hasn't stopped, *this* experience.   it's still going.
& so am i.   even if i can't get there from here: a
diminished fifth, grasping for the rasp that gasps in my
throat, diminuendo.

this was supposed to be an elegy. probably a short one.
(how much can you write about someone you haven't
seen, let alone talked to, for almost ten years?) & it is &
it isn't. i mean it is an elegy, tho it's not "short."
somewhere along the line *james* the poem became *james*
the book. & like all elegies (long or short) it's more
about the writer & the process of writing than about the
elegized. just look at the precursors. ask yourself: who
really remembers edward king & arthur henry hallam?
what does anybody know about *them* that hasn't been
distorted by the numbers, by the filter their elegies are?

& whose mortality is it anyway? the dead i know are the
dead i know. (but i'm the one allergic to sunflower
seeds.)

heliotropes: i figure it's the folks still trying to harness
language that have the problems.

the form of *james* took care of itself — if you're so
inclined.
& yes, don coles' *little bird* is what bob mould would call
"the perfect example." but where the corpus bucked
against the quatrains the corpus won. out of respect, so
to speak, for a little discomfort & shifting. the text
always decomposes in the loam of its bondage.

somewhere along the line i began to accept the tautology:
the elegy as the solipsist's solipsism. *terra damnata*: not a
pretty s/cite. & the megalomaniacal cum messianic
fascination with trying to keep something alive, when
really all it's about is trying to find a better way of
expressing that you're "sorry for their loss." the absence
that apologia is. how i'm effaced: "fully, completely."

& tho i try not to apologize for much anymore, i am sorry. sorry, perhaps, that i wrote this. that i had to. that it will have to be written again.

it's funny — how my words still seem inadequate so long after the fact.   all i know is that between milton & kurt cobain i'm still an "uncouth swain" slurring to make some sense & reparation: "what else should i write / i don't have the right / what else should i be / all apologies."

— *toronto, 18/06/94*